A PORTRAIT OF

Gentleman's Row

ENFIELD PRESERVATION SOCIETY

© Copyright Enfield Preservation Society, 1986

ISBN 0 907318 04 5

Published by Enfield Preservation Society Ltd, 107, Parsonage Lane, Enfield, Middx. EN2 0AB.

Printed by Butler & Tanner Ltd, Frome, Somerset

PUBLISHED TO MARK
THE GOLDEN JUBILEE OF THE
ENFIELD PRESERVATION SOCIETY, 1936–1986

Contents

Foreword

This book was made possible by the late Reginald T. Williams, who lived in Enfield for most of his life and was a talented amateur photographer. Mr Williams was a worshipper and active member of the congregation at Enfield Methodist Church (now Trinity Church) at the corner of Gentleman's Row.

Most of the photographs on the right-hand pages were taken by him, during 1979 and 1980. His purpose was to make a visual record of this much-loved and much-photographed part of Enfield Town. Before his death he gave the photographs to the Enfield Preservation Society, of which he was a Vice-President, in the hope that this book would be published.

The text and the photographs by others have been chosen to provide historical and architectural information which we hope will add to your enjoyment and appreciation of the splendid pictures taken by Mr Williams.

Introduction

Gentleman's Row is a place to be cherished. It lies off Church Street, close to the heart of the town and its busy shops, but is an unspoilt oasis of calm. Elegant and historic buildings from the 17th and 18th centuries look across peaceful gardens to the New River. Charles Lamb stayed here; Royalty were guests.

At one time no street name was needed. The footpath from Church Street to the junction with Holly Walk formed part of the boundary of Enfield Chase, an ancient royal hunting ground. Lamb wrote in 1825 that the house where he was staying was "fifth or sixth on the Chase", which, like Chase Side, was a common name for this small area.

The gardens on the west side of the footpath were encroachments on the Chase, probably encouraged when this small section was cut off from the rest by the New River, an aqueduct built to take water into London in 1611. At the partition of the Chase in 1777, compensation for the encroachments was paid to the Parish of Enfield (see appendix 66).

The name Gentleman's Row (occasionally, Gentleman's Walk) was in use at the beginning of the 19th century, but lapsed and was not formally adopted until towards the century's end. Soon after 1900 the use of the name was extended to include William Place, Belmont Cottages, Rivulet House and Brecon House.

Gentleman's Row is often regarded as a showpiece, but that is not how the individual houses were planned. Most have been lived in continuously for hundreds of years. Generation by generation, they have been enlarged, modernised, rebuilt and altered to meet the style of the times and the needs of their owners. Sometimes the changes have been minimal and harmonious; sometimes, dramatic.

Gentleman's Row now enjoys esteem as a residential area, but this has not always been so. For much of the 19th century it had a somewhat run-down air, and several of the houses were used as schools or boarding-houses.

Three families have done much to preserve the unity of Gentleman's Row. In the 18th century much of it was owned by the Dowbiggin family. From 1864–1952 the Leggatt family owned many of the buildings. More recently there was sympathetic restoration by the Groves family, contributing to the attractive harmony of this jewel in Enfield's heritage.

Looking north along Gentleman's Row

No 1 Gentleman's Row **Public Offices**

This imposing Georgian building was once a private house with grounds extending along Church Street; the lodge at the entrance of its sweeping drive stood opposite the modern Eastern Electricity showrooms. Originally known as Little Park, it had a boating lake where some of the houses in Little Park Gardens now stand.

The picture on page 12 shows the back of the house in about 1880, with Mrs J.B. Muir and family. In 1806 the owner was Admiral Sir Edward Thornbrough, who played a prominent part in the 1794 sea battle of the Glorious First of June, against the French. Other residents have included Dr Kesteven a physician, and Cornelius Walford the actuary, barrister and historian of insurance.

Don Gresswell

The building became known as the Public Offices after it was bought for £4,000 by the Enfield Local Board of Health in 1888. The name Little Park lives on elsewhere – adopted for 5 Gentleman's Row.

In its public life, the building has had many uses. Part of it served as the district's first public library from 1892 until 1911, when the Central Library opened in Cecil Road. Another part was used as a court house until one was built at the bottom of Windmill Hill in 1900.

The house has been owned by successive local authorities, who used it as their principal office until the Civic Centre was opened in Silver Street in 1961. Since then it has had various roles, including Registrar's Office.

A pillar box in front of the Public Offices was removed as an eyesore in 1966.

Enfield Public Library, 1892–1911.

Rear view of the Public Offices, 1979. After major refurbishment by the London Borough of Enfield, costing £546,000, the building re-opened as the Registrar's Office in May 1986.

Mrs J.B. Muir and family in the garden at Little Park.

View towards the house from across the lake.

The lake from the lawn looking east.

Detail of rear of Public Offices showing window canopies.

No 5 Gentleman's Row **Little Park**

The substantial wall in the foreground of the view opposite once hid Hargrave House, a solid Victorian villa built in about 1840.

Public Offices Gentlemans Row, Enfield. C.A.Hodge Enfield. 593

The photograph above shows Hargrave House nestling among trees and almost dwarfed by the Public Offices. Its place was taken in 1927 by an extension to 5 Gentleman's Row. This extension was built to house features removed from Enfield Palace, when it was finally demolished. Now known as the Tudor Room, it is described on the following pages.

The Tudor Room

The picture on this page shows the interior of the Tudor Room, now housed in the building shown opposite. The magnificent stone fireplace bears the royal arms, the crowned Tudor rose, the crowned portcullis and the initials E.R. The room also contains two panels bearing the royal arms and the inscription, in Latin: *The favour of the King is like dew upon the grass.* The ceiling and the fine panelling come from different rooms in the Palace. The windows contain modern stained glass, showing the arms of several queens of England.

Fred French

16

Enfield Palace

Enfield Palace, which once contained the fireplace and other features now in the Tudor Room, Gentleman's Row, stood in Church Street, Enfield, where Pearsons department store is now established. It gives its name to the Palace Gardens shopping precinct, opened in 1982.

Built as a manor house, it was one of the estates of the Duchy of Lancaster, and was still in the ownership of the Crown in Tudor times. Along with New Park, Enfield House (Elsyng) and the manor of Worcesters, it was granted by the young King Edward to his sister Princess Elizabeth in 1550. Enfield tradition closely associates it with the Princess, who was later to become Queen Elizabeth I.

After it passed from royal ownership the Palace had many uses. The engraving opposite shows it towards the end of the 18th century. Dr Robert Uvedale, famous botanist and sometime headmaster of Enfield Grammar School, lived in the Palace and ran his private school there. In the 19th century it again housed a school, at which all five Leggatt brothers were educated. It was later used as a Post Office, until the present Post Office in Church Street was opened in 1906. Just before its demolition it housed the Constitutional Club.

The Cedar, Enfield Palace 1821.

Little Park

Little Park shows how difficult it is to date buildings from their appearance when they have been continually and substantially modified. Nicholas Pevsner described it as "Edwardian" and few would disagree. However, it has been established that the central part dates from Tudor times, and in the second half of the 19th century it had a distinctly "Georgian" appearance. The name Little Park was adopted after it ceased to be used to identify the building which had become the Public Offices.

The house came into the hands of the Leggatt family in 1864. The five Leggatt brothers were well-known in the art world. One married, but the four remaining bachelor brothers lived here for the rest of their lives, playing a prominent and colourful part in Enfield affairs.

The youngest brother, Dudley, the last to die in 1952, kept a scrapbook. A note in this tells us of major alterations to the house at the turn of the century: "The brick exterior of the house . . . is a complete covering of the original building which still stands, although hidden by the more modern structure . . . A piece of stone work, found at the back of some skirting in one of the rooms . . . bears the Tudor Arms, which proves the date of the old building."

The late Queen Mary was often a visitor to Little Park. One visit on 27th February 1920, with Princess Mary (later the Princess Royal), is commemorated by an inscription on the chimney-piece in the drawing-room.

These pictures, taken from the Leggatt scrapbook, show (below) the back of Little Park towards the end of the 19th century, and (opposite) the back of the restored and altered building.

In the garden of Little Park is one of the last traces of another royal residence, considerably more splendid than Enfield Palace or Manor House. It is a weather-vane (shown in the drawing) taken from the Palace of Theobalds, on the northern boundary of Enfield. According to Sir John Summerson, for many years curator of Sir John Soane's Museum, this palace ranked beside Longleat and Burghley as one of the major achievements of Elizabethan building. James I and Charles I used it frequently, and all through the Civil War Parliament kept it in perfect order. After the execution of King Charles I, it was subdivided and sold piecemeal in 1650 and finally demolished.

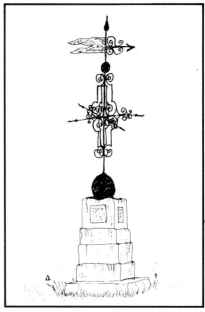

No 7 Gentleman's Row

Number 7 is part of Elm House, described on the next page. It was completed by a modern addition (1955) in part of the former garden of number 5. Its history is, of course, bound up with Elm House. During World War I it was used as a convalescent home for soldiers. The picture shows nurses and soldiers on the flat roof of the hall to number 7. During World War II it was used as a fuel office, and also as sleeping quarters for auxiliary firemen at the fire-station on the site now used as a bus stand opposite The Stag public house.

The flat roof of No 7 as it looks today.

No 9 Gentleman's Row **Elm House**

The original Elm House is now divided between numbers 7 and 9 Gentleman's Row. The name is retained for number 9 which, with some ground floor additions at the rear, is divided into four apartments.

There was a house on this site in the 17th century, but substantial rebuilding took place in the 18th century. One of its more colourful owners during the 18th century was Robert Barnevelt, who was of Dutch descent. His grandfather was apothecary to William III and his father held the same office under George I and George II. He is described as an "eminent cheese-factor and Government contractor" and clearly played a major part in supplying provisions to the armed forces of the Crown.

For many decades before World War I, Elm House was used as a school for girls and little boys and during and after World War I, it had many uses. Members of the 2nd Enfield Girl Guides remember meeting there; they remember, too, the excitement caused by the arrival of HM Queen Mary, who came to see antique furniture stored in the building.

When Elm House was a convalescent home, one of its patients was a soldier later to become the mayor of the municipal borough of Enfield, Alderman A.M. Eeles. A later mayor, Alderman W.H. Cook, remembers sleeping there during his service in the auxiliary fire service in World War II.

Dudley and Percy Leggatt with soldiers and nursing staff outside Elm House.

Elm House gate and railings.

Looking north from Elm House

Originally there were gates and fences between each property on the Gentleman's Row footpath. The last fence to be removed was between Elm House and Fortescue Lodge, sometime after World War II. The photograph above, taken in the mid 1950s, shows its position, although the gate itself had by this time already been removed. A small portion of a fence still remains next to the lamp-post, which now stands on the left.

Facing west across the Chase in 1572 were four houses and one cottage. The first, probably the present Little Park, was owned by Mr Fortescue, and had a garden and orchard of one acre. The next was owned by Thomas Clarke and Richard Wright, with two and a half acres attached. To the north stood a house owned by Sir Thomas Wroth, and beyond was Mr Fortescue's mansion with a garden, orchard and close of three acres.

31

No 11 Gentleman's Row **Fortescue Lodge**

The name Lodge has given rise to the mistaken belief that this house was built as a hunting lodge, perhaps for Sir John Fortescue. In fact it first took the name Fortescue House when Fortescue Hall, a large manor house to its north, was pulled down in 1813. The change to Fortescue Lodge was a Victorian embellishment in the 1870s.

Originally built as an outhouse or stableman's cottage to Fortescue Hall in the 17th century, the rear section was considerably extended early in the 18th century. On the demolition of Fortescue Hall it took over its coach-house and stables, which were retained until this century.

The house is timber-framed with a 19th century stucco facade. The Conservative MP for Enfield, Lt Col R.V.K. Applin, lived here in the 1930s. During World War II the house was used as a billeting station, and was later a doctor's surgery for a time.

Auctioneer's prospectus for Fortescue Lodge.

The Coach House

An excellent example of "upper cruck" construction, the Coach House was originally built as a barn, probably in the 16th century. Later it became the coach-house and stables for Fortescue Hall, and later still for Fortescue Lodge.

Documents show it was twice its current length, but by the 19th century it had been reduced in size to align with the rear wall of Fortescue Lodge. In 1879 it is described as "a coach-house and three-stall stable, knife house, fowl house and large loft over with apple room".

Having fallen into disuse except as a storeroom and become virtually derelict, it was converted into a three-bedroomed house in 1957. The cruck beams (pairs of large curved timbers used as the principal framing of the house) can still be seen in the front part of the upper floor.

Cyril Copp

Coach House before conversion in 1957.

Cyril Copp

Nos 13 and 15 Gentleman's Row
Fortescue Villas

Fortescue Villas are two Victorian houses now divided into four flats. They were built on the site of a large timber-frame house called Fortescue Hall. Although the date 1608 was inscribed above one window of Fortescue Hall, the bulk of the structure certainly predated this. Despite much alteration and extension over the centuries, it was never considered to be a comfortable house and it ended its life as a school before being pulled down in 1813. The land was then used for several decades as a nursery garden until the construction of Fortescue Villas.

At the turn of this century Fortescue Villas housed a girls' school, before being taken over as the Edmonton Board of Guardians' Children's Home.

Watercolour of Fortescue Hall, c.1800.

No 17 Gentleman's Row **Clarendon Cottage**

The irregular 18th-century plaster facade of Clarendon Cottage is much loved by local artists. It is a timber-frame house dating from the 16th and 17th centuries.

By the end of the 17th century it had become, as was the fate of so many houses in Gentleman's Row, a girls' school.

Rear of Clarendon Cottage, late 1940s.

Charles and Mary Lamb

Clarendon Cottage is well-known for its associations with Charles Lamb. In 1825 and again in 1827 Charles Lamb and his sister Mary stayed there with his friends the Allsops. At this time the house was a boarding house run by a Mrs Leishmann. In 1827 Lamb rented a house on Chaseside as he thought that "rural" Enfield would have a beneficial effect on Mary's health.

Charles and Mary Lamb. Portrait by F.S. Cary. Reproduced by courtesy of the National Portrait Gallery.

**The bull's-eye window
was inserted in April 1978.**

No 19 Gentleman's Row **Eastbury**

Sir Albert Richardson, an eminent architect and President of the Royal Academy, expressed his delight in the restoration of this early 18th century house by Major and Mrs Arbuthnot Lane in 1950. As a result the house became a magnet for aspiring architectural students interested in restoration work.

During its restoration, hay (an ancient form of insulation) was found under the roof tiles.

Eastbury was previously known as the School House, because a small Dame School was held in the single storey building in the rear garden. This was reached through a passage, now made into a garage.

The photograph (right) shows the unusual pillared archway and barrel ceiling in the hall.

Harry Sellick

44

No 21 Gentleman's Row **Sedgecope**

This house, formerly known for some years as "Sedgecope", dates back to the 17th century or earlier, although the front is 18th century.

Stanley Smith

The front of Sedgecope, showing the Enfield Preservation Society Listed Building Plaque (see page 71).

The imposing doorcase which enhances Sedgecope's dark red brick front.

Stanley Smith

No 23 Gentleman's Row **Archway House**

Constructed around 1750 this fine building was used as a beer house for many years. It was de-licensed just before World War I and is now known as Archway House. Contemporary with the Public Offices, and not dissimilar, Archway House takes its name from the archway leading to the former Love's Row, now called Chapel Street.

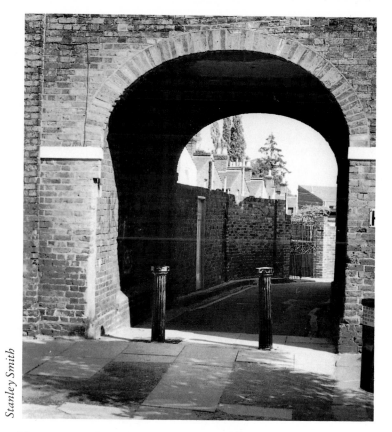

The new metal posts.

Archway from Chapel Street, 1965.

From time to time the arch has been damaged, usually by large vehicles. After pressure by the Enfield Preservation Society and others, the arch was closed in 1978 by strong but ugly posts. At the insistence of the Society, and mainly at its expense, metal posts of a more attractive design have been substituted. It is understood that the new design is now to be standard in suitable places throughout the London Borough of Enfield.

The houses in Holly Walk facing the playing fields were built on the orchard and garden of the Archway Tavern, which included a skittle alley. The first three houses in Holly Walk nearest to Archway House were once called Archway Cottages.

49

No 25 Gentleman's Row

This house, mainly 19th century and at one stage the stables for the Archway Tavern, was for many years a general shop in the village tradition. It survived well into the supermarket era, eventually closing in the late 1960s.

Under the left-hand window of Archway House can be seen the trap-door through which barrels of beer reached the cellar of the then Archway Tavern.

Shop front, early 1960s.

Don Gresswell

Nos 27–33 and 35–45 Gentleman's Row

These two photographs show the northern end of Gentleman's Row. Unusually, they show no cars – with the co-operation of local residents and others, the cars which normally line both sides of the road were removed one Sunday morning while these pictures were taken.

The picture above shows houses on the eastern side. The four early 19th century houses on the right (Nos 27–33) are listed as being of particular interest; the rest (Nos 35–45) bear a plaque stating "William Place 1871". The picture (right) shows houses (Nos 18–28) called "Belmont Cottages" on the western side of the road. This terrace of six houses was built in the 1890s. They filled the gap between The Haven (No 16) and Rivulet House (No 32).

Nos 2, 4, 6, 8 Gentleman's Row

A well-loved subject for local artists, these cottages form a charming group facing south, unlike the rest of the houses in Gentleman's Row which all face east or west. Once called River Cottages, they were built in the late 18th century after the Parish of Enfield had sold the encroachment of land from Enfield Chase on which they stand.

Nos 2, 4, 6, 8 photographed in 1985.

Mary Soulsby

Nos 10, 12, 14, 16 Gentleman's Row

Numbers 10, 12, 14 and 16 back onto the New River. Formerly the four occupants had "dipping rights" which enabled them to use the New River as a water supply. By about 1865 the first three had a mains water supply, leaving only No 16 dependent on the New River. The gate at the rear of No 16, "The Haven", which enabled water to be brought from the New River by bucket is still to be seen, as the picture overleaf shows.

The cottage in the inset photograph shows 14 Gentleman's Row as it was in 1968. Over 300 years old, it had been a farm bothy, part storehouse, tool shed and living quarters for a farm labourer. It was pulled down in 1970 and replaced by the house shown in the picture opposite.

Nos 10 and 12 on the left of this picture were once known as Nos 1 and 2 Hope Cottages.

Stanley Smith

No 16 Gentleman's Row **The Haven**

It is thought that this pretty house originally faced the New River, with the back of the house (now its front) being some 300 years old. When it was extended in brick a century or so later, the main entrance was relocated in its present position.

This house also seems to have been used as a school at some stage.

Stanley Smith

Rear view of The Haven.

No 32 Gentleman's Row **Rivulet House**

Originally called Rivulet Cottage, this house was probably built in the early 19th century. The front of the house formerly faced over the New River, and to appreciate its well-proportioned features it should be viewed from the rear. It is probable that the garden at one time stretched down to The Haven (No. 16), as Belmont Cottages were built on land owned by the occupier of Rivulet House.

Among former residents of Rivulet House was Thirza Jonckheere-Cox, founder of the Enfield and Edmonton Art Circle. She is commemorated by a circular seat surrounding a tree between Gentleman's Row and the New River.

Mary Soulsby

Rear view of Rivulet House.

No 55 Gentleman's Row **Brecon House**

A mid-18th century gentleman's residence, No 55 was altered at the rear during the 19th century. For many years it has been the last of its period in the immediate locality, complete with stables and standing in its original grounds.

In 1985 the house, which had fallen into a bad state of repair, was restored by its new owner, Mr A.B. Webster. Although the future of Brecon House has been safeguarded, the fate of its back garden is unsettled, as this land is in separate ownership. Planning permission to build houses on the land has twice been refused by Enfield council; public inquiries subsequently upheld both refusals.

After the second inquiry in November 1984, the Inspector appointed by the Department of the Environment reported: "In my opinion Brecon House is a building of sufficient architectural and historical importance to require more space about it than would be provided. . . It would be most unfortunate for the long term future of Brecon House and for the Conservation Area, if at this stage, when after a period of uncertainty, the property is being thoroughly restored, it were to be deprived of an appropriate setting."

Mary Soulsby

Brecon House: Wall and Gate

Walls, and fences of wrought iron or cast iron, figure importantly among features which have prompted the Department of the Environment to list much of Gentleman's Row as being of special architectural or historic interest. This recently restored wall to Brecon House is a good example. It marks the end of Gentleman's Row.

Mary Soulsby

Appendix

Encroachments

The encroachments around the edge of the Chase, not only at Enfield, but at Southgate, Winchmore Hill, Cockfosters, Monken Hadley, Potters Bar and other places, had existed for centuries. Those that held them paid a small rent to the parish of Enfield but on the enclosure of the Chase in 1777 the freehold was sold to the occupier at 30 and 50 times the copyhold rent.

According to the *Story of Enfield Chase* by David Pam, plots 96–101 represent the front gardens of the houses now called Gentleman's Row. In 1769 details of encroachments include the following:

87.	Mrs Mary Capener (Brecon House) House Offices, yard and garden	32 perches
88.	Garden opposite	20 perches
92.	Mr William Rout. House and Garden	24 perches
93.	Mr Henry Warren. Two houses and garden	34 perches
94.	Mrs Barnes. House and Garden	23 perches
95.	Mrs Archer. House and Garden	21 perches
96.	Mr Samuel Dowbiggin. The enclosure before the four Houses	1 rood 6 perches
97.	Miss Jenks. Enclosure before the House	18 perches
98.	Mr Robert Barnevelt. Enclosure before the four houses	1 rood 31 perches
99.	Mr Clarke. Enclosure before the house	28 perches
100.	Mr Frederick Maurer. Enclosure before the house	1 rood 9 perches
101.	Mr Frederick Maurer. Three houses gardens etc.	34 perches

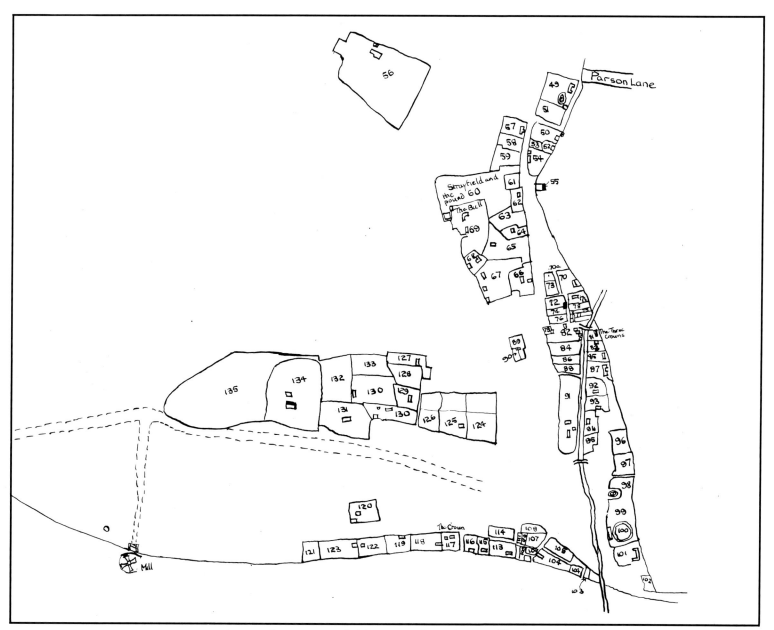

Encroachments at Enfield Town and Windmill Hill in 1769.

Stanley Smith

The front gardens of the houses in Gentleman's Row.

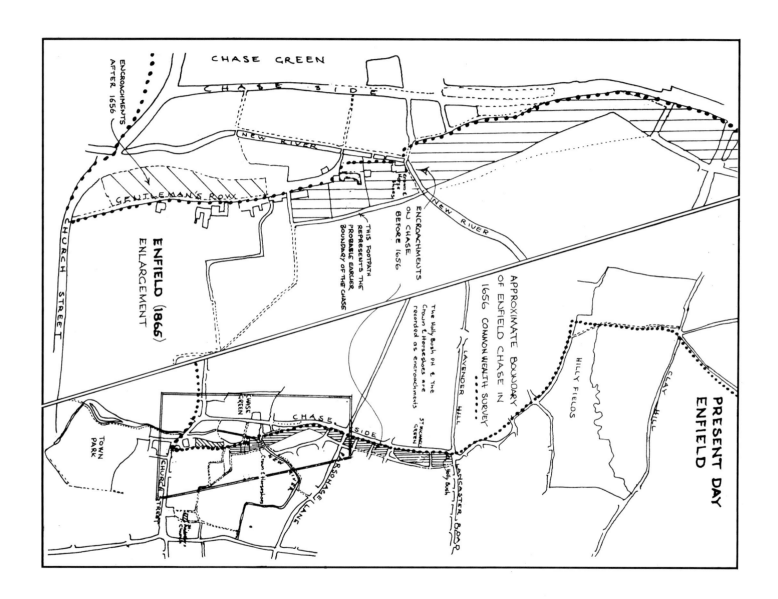

CHASE GREEN

ENCROACHMENTS AFTER 1656

CHASE SIDE

NEW RIVER

NEW RIVER

GENTLEMAN'S ROW

CHURCH STREET

ENFIELD (1865) ENLARGEMENT

THIS FOOTPATH REPRESENTS THE PROBABLE EARLIER BOUNDARY OF THE CHASE

ENCROACHMENTS ON CHASE BEFORE 1656

APPROXIMATE BOUNDARY OF ENFIELD CHASE IN 1656 COMMONWEALTH SURVEY

The Holly Bush PH & The Crown & Horseshoes are recorded as encroachments

HILLY FIELDS

CLAY HILL

PRESENT DAY ENFIELD

LAVENDER HILL

TOWN PARK

CHASE GREEN

CHASE SIDE

CHURCH STREET

PARSONAGE LANE

LANCASTER ROAD

ST MICHAEL'S CRESC

Crown & Horseshoes

Holly Bush

Conservation Areas

Gentleman's Row lies within Enfield Town Conservation Area, which extends from Chase Green in the west to Enfield Town station in the east. Comprising most of the town centre, St Andrew's Parish Church, Enfield Grammar School, Silver Street, Chase Green and part of Chase Side, this was the first of the 12 conservation areas to be designated in the London Borough of Enfield.

Gentleman's Row itself has been given the rare status of Outstanding Conservation Area. To protect this historic street from piecemeal alterations which could ruin its unique character, Enfield Council obtained special powers from the Department of the Environment to make an Article 4 Direction. Under this Direction detailed planning approval must be sought for alterations to any building, for exterior painting, and for the erection of walls, fences, sheds and various other front garden features.

Conservation area legislation gives the Local Planning Authority powers to ensure that new building in the area is sympathetic to its surroundings. It also controls the demolition of buildings (including fences, walls, gates and railings), and the felling or lopping of trees. The main purpose of the legislation is to protect the special character of the area, and to ensure that when changes are made, the quality of the heritage is maintained.

Listed Buildings

Most of the buildings in Gentleman's Row are listed by the Department of the Environment for their special architectural and historic interest, and are classified as Grade II.
The criteria for listing are: all buildings built before 1700 which survive in anything like their original condition; most buildings of 1700 to 1840; buildings of definite quality and character between 1840 and 1914. Selected buildings of 1914 to 1939 are also considered.

Many of the houses in Gentleman's Row bear a plaque like the one below. Householders display this to indicate that their house has been listed by the Department of Environment for its special architectural or historic interest.

These plaques can be seen on houses in many parts of Enfield. They have been produced by the Enfield Preservation Society to encourage interest in our civic heritage.

The Enfield Listed Building Plaque designed for Enfield Preservation Society by Mrs Mahala Hill.

Acknowledgements

This book could not have been made without the willing help of many people.

We are especially indebted to the photographers who have taken pictures for us or allowed us to use their prints. Our thanks to Mary Soulsby, to Stanley Smith and to Olive Sellick who allowed us to use the work of her husband, the late Harry Sellick. Other photographs were helpfully provided or arranged by Cyril Copp, Fred French, Don Gresswell and Kevin Hinds.

Hugh Leggatt, head of the family business of Leggatt Bros, fine art dealers of St. James's, generously allowed us to copy pictures from his family scrapbook.

We thank the local history section of the London Borough of Enfield, and Graham Dalling in particular, for the loan of photographs and documents. The portraits of Charles and Mary Lamb are reproduced by courtesy of the National Portrait Gallery. The map of 1866 appears by permission of the British Library.

We are grateful to Alan Skilton for the panorama of Gentleman's Row on the front endpapers and for the encroachment map, and to Francis Fitzpatrick for the sketch of the weathervane in the garden of Little Park.

Finally we thank all members of the council of management of Enfield Preservation Society, with special reference to David Pam, a tower of strength on historical matters, also our chairman Valerie Carter and her immediate predecessor Alan Skilton, for their encouragement and the exercise of their professional skills.

We also thank Marks and Spencer for their sponsorship.

We hope we have not inadvertently omitted any names from this list of those who have assisted us, and to whom we acknowledge our considerable gratitude.

Claire Hansen, Honor Head, Irene Smith, Donald Potter, David Roberts